AUDIO ACCESS & FLUTE BOOKLET INCLUDED

T0195276

FLUTE • PIANO

SUNDAY SOLOS
FOR FLUTE

Arranged & Orchestrated by Larry Moore

NOTE: See flute booklet for instructions to access audio tracks online.

ISBN 978-1-4803-9973-0

HAL•LEONARD®
CORPORATION
7777 W. BLUEMOUND RD. P.O. BOX 13819 MILWAUKEE, WI 53213

Visit Hal Leonard Online at
www.halleonard.com

COME, THOU ALMIGHTY KING

Traditional
Music by FELICE de GIARDINI

HOW GREAT IS OUR GOD

Words and Music by CHRIS TOMLIN,
JESSE REEVES and ED CASH

PRAISE HIM! PRAISE HIM!

Words by FANNY J. CROSBY
Music by CHESTER G. ALLEN

10,000 REASONS
(Bless the Lord)

Words and Music by JONAS MYRIN
and MATT REDMAN

AMAZING GRACE
(My Chains Are Gone)

Words by JOHN NEWTON
Traditional American Melody
Additional Words and Music by CHRIS TOMLIN
and LOUIE GIGLIO

BECAUSE HE LIVES

Words and Music by WILLIAM J. GAITHER
and GLORIA GAITHER

SUNDAY SOLOS
FOR FLUTE

Arranged & Orchestrated by Larry Moore

Tuning notes (B♭ and A) are included in the online audio tracks.

To access audio visit:
www.halleonard.com/mylibrary

Enter Code
7841-6873-9986-6583

HAL•LEONARD®
CORPORATION
7777 W. BLUEMOUND RD. P.O. BOX 13819 MILWAUKEE, WI 53213

COME, THOU ALMIGHTY KING

Flute

Traditional
Music by FELICE de GIARDINI

10,000 REASONS
(Bless the Lord)

Flute

Words and Music by JONAS MYRIN
and MATT REDMAN

HOW GREAT IS OUR GOD

Flute

Words and Music by CHRIS TOMLIN,
JESSE REEVES and ED CASH

PRAISE HIM! PRAISE HIM!

Flute

Words by FANNY J. CROSBY
Music by CHESTER G. ALLEN

AMAZING GRACE
(My Chains Are Gone)

Words by JOHN NEWTON
Traditional American Melody
Additional Words and Music by CHRIS TOMLIN
and LOUIE GIGLIO

Flute

BECAUSE HE LIVES

Flute

Words and Music by WILLIAM J. GAITHER
and GLORIA GAITHER

I LOVE TO TELL THE STORY

Flute

Words by A. CATHERINE HANKEY
Music by WILLIAM G. FISCHER

WHAT A FRIEND WE HAVE IN JESUS

Flute

Words by JOSEPH M. SCRIVEN
Music by CHARLES C. CONVERSE

I SING THE MIGHTY POWER OF GOD

Flute

Words by ISAAC WATTS
Music from *Gesangbuch der Herzogl*

LEAD ON, O KING ETERNAL

Words by ERNEST W. SHURTLEFF
Music by HENRY T. SMART

Flute

SING TO THE KING

Flute

Words and Music by
BILLY JAMES FOOTE

WE BOW DOWN

Flute

Words and Music by
TWILA PARIS

I LOVE TO TELL THE STORY

Words by A. CATHERINE HANKEY
Music by WILLIAM G. FISCHER

33

Bring out melody

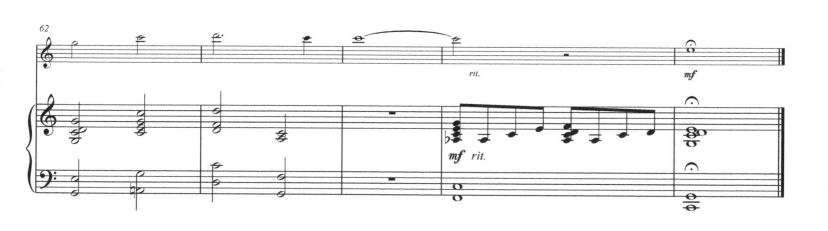

WHAT A FRIEND WE HAVE IN JESUS

Words by JOSEPH M. SCRIVEN
Music by CHARLES C. CONVERSE

I SING THE MIGHTY POWER OF GOD

Words by ISAAC WATTS
Music from *Gesangbuch der Herzogl*

LEAD ON, O KING ETERNAL

Words by ERNEST W. SHURTLEFF
Music by HENRY T. SMART

WE BOW DOWN

Words and Music by
TWILA PARIS

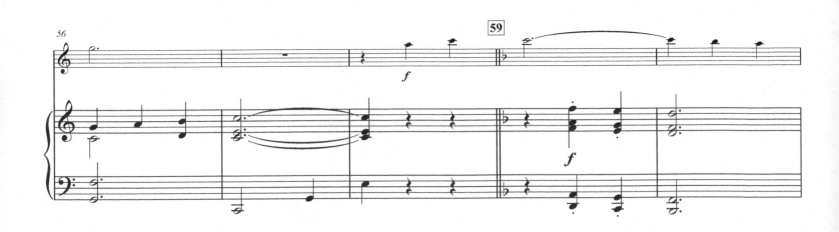

SING TO THE KING

Words and Music by
BILLY JAMES FOOTE